ON SOME MEANS OF GAINING

RELIGIOUS AND MORAL INFLUENCE

OVER BOYS;

A PAPER,

READ

BY THE REV. W. J. CONYBEARE,

AT THE FIRST

EDUCATIONAL MEETING OF THE MASTERS

OF THE

COLLEGIATE SCHOOLS,

OCTOBER 8 1844,

AND NOW PRIVATELY PRINTED FOR THEIR USE.

———————

LIVERPOOL:
WAREING WEBB, CASTLE-STREET.

ON SOME

MEANS OF GAINING MORAL INFLUENCE
OVER THE CHARACTER OF BOYS.

AT this our first meeting to discuss subjects bearing on our professional duty,* I think no topic can more appropriately engage our attention than the question, How we may most effectually make our work in reality, what it is in name, Education, as distinguished from mere teaching; in other words, how we may gain such an influence over our pupils, as to educate their hearts, affections, and consciences, as well as to instruct their understandings. We are all agreed that this is our great object, and most wretched would it be to think otherwise —most miserable to imagine ourselves merely engaged in pouring a certain quantum of knowledge into the brain, instead of co-operating in the Christian work of moulding the character, and influencing the life, of our fellow-Christians,——the task of preparing those committed to our care, not merely for their earthly, but for their heavenly calling.

It is needless, however, to dwell on this, since no

* I subjoin, at the end of this Paper, the Circular with which these meetings commenced, in order that each Master may have a copy of it in his hands.

B

one among us can dispute that which forms the fundamental principle from which our existence as an Educational body has sprung. Without further introduction, therefore, I will give the substance of a few practical hints which I have thrown together, as to the best means of realising that which we all wish and intend.

For the sake of fixing our ideas, let us consider the means which we possess of influencing the boys rightly, during the course of a common school-day, and in school hours.

The morning begins with our all meeting, Masters and Boys alike, under one roof, to join in common prayer. How much of the impressiveness of such a meeting upon the minds of the boys, will depend on the manner in which they observe us to regard it. The deepest solemnity and reverence should of course mark our whole manner, in going in and coming out from prayers: and this is even more necessary, because, unhappily, the character of the Building in which we meet for public worship, is not such as of itself to add to the solemnity of the occasion. Again, if we all join *audibly* in the responses, it will manifestly be a great inducement to the Boys to do so likewise. Moreover, if we observe any instance of misconduct in the classes which come under our respective care, during the time of prayers, we should be most careful never to pass it over, but to shew the offender how much hurt and grieved we feel at the dishonour done to God.

The next act of the day is the reading of the

Bible with the boys, and explaining it to them. This (according to the manner in which it is done,) may be a mere form, or a true means of religious education. In the first place, it would perhaps be well, after the boys are seated, to insist upon perfect silence in the room, and make a solemn pause before beginning to read, in order to shew our feeling of the reverence due to the words about to be read. The general rule with regard to the chapter to be read, namely, that it should be the second lesson for the Morning Service, should of course be strictly observed, except in one or two of the senior classes of all, in which a more entirely continuous course may be sometimes preferable. But I think it is not necessary that the *whole* chapter should always be read; this should rather depend on the nature of its contents. If they are such as to require much explanation, it is better only to read a part, and explain that fully; or again, if they naturally lead to inferences directly applicable to boys, such an opportunity should not be passed over, of pointing out, in the kindest tone and manner, the thoughts on which we should wish them especially to dwell. Above all, we should be careful, by frequent questions, and by requiring a full explanation of the meaning of what is read, to prevent this reading of the Bible from degenerating into a mere mechanical repetition of unheeded words.

Supposing the day to be Monday, the saying of the Sunday's Divinity Lesson will be the next directly religious employment in which the class is engaged;

but there is less need to dwell on this, because the spirit in which such lessons should be heard, is precisely the same with that which should prevail during the reading of the Bible; I think, however, that on both these occasions we cannot be too careful that our manner should correspond with our feelings of affectionate interest in the religious welfare of those whom we are teaching. At such times a harsh and unkind manner would be especially out of place, and certain to destroy all chance of usefulness.

The school day concludes with evening prayers, about which the same remarks may be made as with regard to morning prayers. The difference, however, in the size of the room makes one caution desirable, in order that the performance of the service should be perfectly reverent; namely, that the boys should be reminded, from time to time, that the tone in which their responses should be made must not be too loud, and especially that no one boy should let his voice be heard above the rest.

Having thus considered the portion of the day given up directly to religion, let us now consider our intercourse with the boys during the time of common lessons. How may we make their employment during this, the largest portion of their time, subservient to their true, that is, their moral education?

First, I think, by the enforcing of perfect obedience, and orderly and respectful conduct. Without this, it is of course impossible that they should learn any thing; but it is far more impossible that they should receive moral good, from a system in which habits of submission and self-restraint could not be gained. We should (I am convinced) think no regulations too minute, which may have a tendency to keep up that systematic discipline which is the safeguard of these good habits. And nothing can excuse us, if we allow a single instance of disobedience or disorder to go unpunished.

Another most important moral habit which true education has for its object to foster, is that of industry. We should be careful to represent persevering application to our boys as their positive duty, and idleness as their besetting sin; and we take far too low a ground, if we ever suffer ourselves to speak of it merely as their *interest* to acquire such habits, because they cannot succeed in life without them. This may be very well as a subsidiary motive, and as such it is used by Providence; but we ought never to impress it upon our pupils alone; we ought not to forget to tell them, that while they cannot get on in the world without perseverance, it is equally true, and far more important, that they cannot get to heaven without it. It is by thus always bringing forward the higher, and not the lower motives of action; by shewing that we take Christian, and not Heathen views of life and of its objects, that we may hope to make the tone of thought and feeling among our boys higher than that which would have prevailed among a set of Roman or Athenian school-boys. In this particular matter of industry, we ought especially to keep an eye on the individual character of the boy, and make the greatest possible difference between wilful idleness and natural stupidity; nor can I fancy a case in which we ought to shew more kindness than when we find a stupid boy really exerting himself.

Another way in which we may encourage or depress a high moral feeling among the boys, is by our mode of regarding their statements of facts. If we seem always to listen to their assertions with suspicion, and shew them that we have no confidence in their veracity, we are in fact doing our best to encourage them in habitual lying. If, on the other hand, we always assume that they speak the truth, except when they are actually proved to do the contrary, we shall call out their sense of honour to aid their conscience; for any but a thoroughly depraved boy will feel it a shame to deceive a master who trusts him.* No doubt, in some cases, this conduct will leave us under deception; but it is a far smaller evil that we should be sometimes taken in, than that we should lower the feeling of honour in the School; and we may (I think) depend upon it, that if we treat the boys as Christian gentlemen, we shall by degrees make them approach that character.

Connected with this subject, is the tone we should assume with regard to tale-bearing among the boys; this should always be discountenanced, for no boy ever informs against another from a pure motive, and he always violates his own sense of honour in doing so. For this reason, I would never act on information given by one boy against another, nor ever attempt

---

* So the Rugby boys used to say, " It is a shame to tell Arnold a lie— he always believes one."

to learn anything by such means, except in investigations of a strictly judicial character. A strong reason against doing so (besides those already mentioned,) is that such a practice destroys kindliness of feeling among the boys themselves, which we ought to endeavour, as far as in us lies, to promote, and to represent as a Christian duty.

The last thing I will add about our work in school hours, is that we may sometimes take advantage of some of the lessons to increase our knowledge of the individual characters of our pupils; one may occasionally set boys, by way of English composition, to write an account of their employments in the holidays, or of a day at home, &c., with this object. All such plans are good, when not carried so far as to wear an appearance of inquisitiveness.

These are the principal points which occur to me, in which we may make our intercourse with our classes in school subservient to the true end of our profession. But I think that no master who really has this high end for his main object, will limit his intercourse with his pupils to that which he can have in the school-room. He will endeavour to gain a stronger influence over them, and to win their personal regard, by seeing as much as he can of them out of school also. The opportunities we have of doing this will be no doubt various; but I think all of us might do it in some degree, and none without doing good by it. Of course we ought to make such intercourse as agreeable to the boys as we possibly can; and how to do this is rather a difficult question. One good way, I should think, would be to take them excursions into the country, to Chester, or elsewhere. Another, to invite some of the more advanced to read with us on some particular subjects. If in this way we are so happy as to gain the confidence of any boy, we shall then be able to take opportunities of urging upon him, with much more advantage, important Christian duties, and perhaps shall put him in the way of visiting the poor and sick, of teaching in Sunday Schools, or in some other way of breaking through the spell of that life of mere selfishness which is so natural to us all.

Thus much I think all School-masters may do; but I am well aware, that from those among us who are not only School-masters, but Clergymen, still more is required. Undoubtedly our ordination vows cannot require less of us, than that we should consider the charge committed to us as a cure of souls; unquestionably our relation to those boys who come more immediately into connexion with us, is the same as that between a parochial minister and his flock. Perjured we certainly are, if we do not use all our efforts to train for heaven the souls committed to our guidance. For this great object we may use all the means hitherto enumerated, in common with the other masters; and we may add to them, I think, with advantage, intercourse of a more directly and professedly religious kind. The best method which has yet occurred to me, is that we should have a few boys to come to us regularly on Sundays, and should

carry on with them some definite course of reading
suited to their age. We should always, I think,
choose for such a purpose, a subject which is devotional and practical, rather than dogmatical. As an
instance of the sort of books suitable for the purpose,
I may mention Walton's Lives,—the Life of Bishop
Wilson,—many of the lives in Wordsworth's Eccle-
siastical Biography,—the Lives of the Port Royalists,
—parts of Law's "Call to a Devout Life,"—Bishop
Short on Christianity,—some of Abbott's works, (which
latter are far better read to boys than put into their
hands, because thus an opportunity is given of leaving
out, or of censuring, the parts which are disfigured
by a tone of irreverence,) and above all, Dr. Arnold's
Sermons.* I cannot mention these last without
expressing my strong feeling that every schoolmaster
in the country ought to have both the sermons and
the life of that great man daily in his hands, and in
his heart,—I am sure nothing can be more likely to
stimulate us to a conscientious discharge of duty,
than to see how all the energies of such a mind were
devoted to his work, which is also ours. And if it
might be that some portion of his spirit should so be

* Another very good subject for Sunday reading with our boys, would
be the lives of Missionaries; and this many be made extremely interesting
to them, by means of maps, pictures, descriptions of scenery and national
character, &c. If we could awake in the minds even of a few of the
future merchants of this place, an earnest desire to co-operate in spreading
the knowledge of Christianity among the heathen, we might hope that
the seed here sown would bear fruit in the farthest ends of the earth.

kindled in our hearts, we need not despair of usefulness in some degree proportionate to his.

At these Sunday meetings, we might, besides the reading, which would form their main business, have private interviews with the different boys who came to us, by keeping one, every now and then, after the rest were gone. At such interviews we should have the opportunity, as occasions seemed to present themselves for doing so judiciously,* of enforcing the duty of self-examination and other religious habits; and of recommending the use of such books as Bishop Kenn's Manual of Prayers for Winchester School,

---

* On this point I subjoin an extract from a letter received by me from a friend, who is a Master in one of our Public Schools. " Unless a boy has been religiously brought up, I am convinced that an exhortation, if not grounded on some action or event, is completely a pearl cast before a swine, and is always denominated ' a *jaw*.' Nay, even with boys well brought up, to be of any use, they must be very rare, and short. The other day a boy, whom I know very well, and like very much, and who has decided religious feelings, told me, that in spite of trying his best, he did badly in his form. Amongst other pieces of advice, I recommended him to make such difficulties a subject of prayer, and said a few words on this point. He seemed struck, promised that he would, and was plainly interested. Last Sunday, without any handle at all, I began talking to him generally on these subjects, and all that I got was a tired and vacant look, and no reply at all.

" With regard to indirect modes of influence, I am sure that kindness is one of the greatest, as leading them to feel something like affection for you, and therefore disposing them to prize what you say. How powerful an engine *love* is, in producing strong religious feeling, and exertion for the good of others, is shown in the language of St. Paul to the Thessalonians and Corinthians. We cannot wonder that he laboured for them as he did, when he felt to them as a father or a brother. Nor can we wonder that they tried to do what would please him, when they were treated by him with such overpowering affection. Hence, to try and stir up in our hearts a feeling of affection to the boys, and by our behaviour to them to produce a return of it, seems a great indirect means of religious good."

or the more recent collection of Prayers and Self-examinations published for the use of Rugby School.

There is one caution with reference to such meetings which should not be lost sight of, viz., the importance of letting the parents of the boys who attend, know exactly at what time they ought to expect the return of their sons. It is also a good thing to make the boys bring, on each Sunday, a short analysis of what was read on the Sunday before, and to look over this with them, one by one, after the reading is over, in a separate room. Thus they are dismissed *separately*, which is a great point gained; because, if they all go away together, there is a great chance of all serious impressions being dissipated as soon as they leave the house.

Those among our number who take Boarders, have, in addition to that which they share with the rest of us, a superadded field of usefulness. Placed as they are in the position of parents, they have the power of carrying out the idea of education in its fullest extent. I will not, however, venture to dwell on a responsibility which is (I am sure) so fully felt, but will only offer one practical hint, drawn from my own experience. When I was a school-boy, no day in the week was so ill spent by myself and my school-fellows as Sunday. We had nothing to do, and employed the idle time in reading novels or in quarrelling. I am sure that if a good supply of suitable books had been provided for us, many of us would have spent our time more profitably. And I cannot but think that it should be one of the first objects in the management of a boarding-house, to provide a good supply of Sunday-books, the use of which might perhaps not be allowed on any other day. Of course these books should not be dry essays on Divinity, but such as boys would naturally read with pleasure. For example, the lives of good men, either real or imaginary; and such religious works of fiction as tend to enlist the imagination and affections on the side of religion; the latter I think of especial importance, and likely to be most useful to the young. I may mention the following as valuable books (suited to boys of different ages,) for the above-mentioned purpose, in addition to those recommended above (p. 11):

Hannah More's Tracts.
Archdeacon Wilberforce's Allegories.
Father Clement.
Shadow of the Cross (Burns).
Autobiography of John Newton.
Barber's Missionary Tales (Nisbet).
Amy Herbert.
Emma and her Nurse.
Sherwood's Lady of the Manor.
———————— Fairchild Family.
Abbott's Hoaryhead, and other Stories.
Pilgrim's Progress (Southey's edition).
Tracts published by Christian Knowledge Society.*

* The fullest information with regard to the publications of the Christian Knowledge Society may be found in their Catalogue of Books, published annually, and very well arranged. The Catalogue of the Tract Society may also be consulted with advantage, as, although some of their publications are objectionable, many are very good. I may mention one

Carne's Lives of Eminent Missionaries (Fisher).
Life of Wilberforce (abridged edition).
Life of Felix Neff.
Life of Oberlin.
Southey's Life of Wesley.
Hone's Lives of Eminent Christians (Christian Kn. Society.)
Life of Francke (Seeley).
Life of H. Kirk White, by Southey.
Taylor's Hymns for Infant Minds.
Keble's Christian Year.
Evans's Stories of the Early British Church.
———— Scripture Biography.
Sketches of Christianity in Northern India (Seeley).
Missionary Sketches in Southern India, by S. T. (Nisbet).
Night of Toil (Hatchard).
First Missionary Book for the Young (Tract Society).
The Church in the Colonies (parts) Society for Prop. Gospel.
English Missions (in parts).   Do.
Church Missionary Gleaner (in numbers), Ch. Miss. Society.
Lives of the Apostles and Evangelists (Christian Kn. Society.
Scripture Topography   Do.
Extracts from Travellers   Do.
Pierre and his Family, a Huguenot narrative.
Heber's Journal (Murray, Home and Col. Library).
Richmond's Annals of the Poor.
Howard's Scripture History.
Krummacher's Infant Saviour (Wertheim).
Wanderings of the Israelites (Tract Society).
Miracles of our Lord (Tract Society).
Churchman's Monthly Companion, in parts (Rivington.)

One thing is most important to recollect, with regard to such books, viz., that provided their contents are such as to awaken devotional feelings and

(by name Lucy Morley,) as one of the most beautiful stories I ever read. I must also specify Prasca Loupouloff (the original of the " Exiles of Siberia,") published by the Christian Knowledge Society.

religious earnestness in the heart, it matters little
what opinions on subjects of controversial theology
they may express. For all such passages will be
either passed over by boys altogether, or interpreted
in accordance with their previous teaching.

Another part of each Sunday might be well spent,
in a boarding-house, in helping the boys to prepare
their divinity lesson for the next day, intelligently
and devotionally.

I cannot conclude these few hints on so important
a subject, more appropriately than by reading an
extract from a paper read by Dr. Blochmann at the
annual meeting of the School-masters of Saxony, held
at Dresden, in the spring of this year, which will, I
am sure, be interesting to us all, not only for its
intrinsic beauty, but also for the light which it throws
upon the feelings of our professional brethren in
Germany. The original paper itself is in our Library,
being one of the educational documents brought from
Germany by Mr. Howson. Dr. Blochmann's words
are as follows :—

" We share with parents a very high calling ; and,
" alas ! we too often lose sight of what ought to be the
" chief end of our labours. Can there be a happier
" profession than to be surrounded by the opening
" minds of children, and to give to them, according as
" they can receive it, of our accumulated knowledge
" and experience ? It is refreshing to have the care
" of a garden full of spring flowers,— to pluck up the
" weeds which would choke them, and supply them

" with the pure stream which their life needs for its
" sustenance. But what are all the gardens of this
" earth, compared to the garden which we enter afresh
" every morning, full of Heaven's own flowers,—rich
" in the seeds of eternal life, which are appointed not
" only to blossom here, but through all eternity?
" What position can be more happy and blessed than
" ours, in the midst of our children, who look up to
" us for instruction and nourishment, whereby they
" may grow in all wisdom and goodness? If we do
" not feel ourselves blessed, is it not our own fault?
" If we are continually complaining of trouble and
" labour, are not such complaints called forth solely
" because we 'love little,' and our hearts and spirits
" are deadened?

"My brethren in this high calling, let us go forth
" each morning into our youthful world in Christ's
" name, and in the might of His Spirit, and wherever
" we see a heart uncleansed from impure desires, let
" us work with all our soul that it may be purified;
" if we behold any one following crooked ways, let us
" draw him to the straight paths of righteousness; if
" one weary and weak in spirit, let us strengthen
" him; if one fallen away through carelessness and
" self-confidence, let us earnestly endeavour to awake
" the power of conscience within him. Let us learn
" from the teaching of our Master, Christ, how to
" regain lost souls, how they may be purified and
" cleansed, how the weak may be strengthened, and
" how true spiritual life may be supplied. Christ

" spoke of the things of eternal life, and His words
" are sufficient for the healing of the whole of man-
" kind, how long soever they may have wandered in
" the region and shadow of death.

" Our deeds, words, and feelings, should be the
" influences wherewith we should nourish the hearts
" of our children. But no one can give more than
" he has, therefore it is clear that the state of our
" own hearts will greatly affect that of those under
" our care, and that all precepts on the subject may
" be included in this one sentence, 'keep thy own
" heart rightly, and thou wilt then be enabled rightly
" to keep, and to mould, the hearts of others.' We
" know that it is impossible to make our pupils feel
" the influence of what is good, and noble, and
" beautiful upon earth, if we ourselves do not feel it;
" how much more impossible, then, to influence them
" in spiritual things, unless our hearts are enlightened
" and sanctified. It is only when the word of God
" is living in our hearts, which tells us that 'Christ
" is the true bread from heaven, and is given for the
" life of the world,' and when we, through the obedi-
" ence of faith, are in constant communion with the
" Giver of this life,—it is only then that this word
" which we teach can have a real living influence
" upon our children's hearts; for only living faith
" awakens faith, and spirit cannot be kindled but by
" spirit."

———————————

GENERAL CIRCULAR

SUMMONING THE FIRST OF THE EDUCATIONAL MEETINGS,

9TH SEPTEMBER, 1844.

THE Principal, considering that the schools have now arrived at sufficient maturity to give those employed in their management some experience in the working of the system of education which has been established, is of opinion that the time is come when much benefit might be derived from the discussion, between his colleagues and himself, of subjects bearing upon their common professional duties as schoolmasters. He therefore proposes that meetings for this purpose should be held from time to time, not less often than once a month, and that they should begin by the reading of a short paper on some educational subject, to be followed by a conversation either on the subject of the paper, or upon any other educational topics which those present may be inclined to bring forward. A few of those points which would most naturally form the subject of such discussions are appended to this circular, but of course they are not meant to be exclusive, but are only given as specimens.

In conclusion, the Principal begs to invite those Masters who feel inclined to take an interest in the discussion of similar questions, to meet on Tuesday, October 8, at seven o'clock in the evening, when the

ADDRESSES.

www.ingramcontent.com/pod-product-compliance
Lightning Source LLC
Chambersburg PA
CBHW082058070426
42452CB00052B/2733